SCIENCE FICTION TO SCIENCE FACT

TRACTOR BEAMS

BY HOLLY DUHIG

ANALYSIS OF THE SOURCE FILE

Gareth Stevens
PUBLISHING

Please visit our website, **www.garethstevens.com**.
For a free color catalog of all our high-quality books,
call toll free 1-800-542-2595 or fax 1-877-542-2596.

Cataloging-in-Publication Data
Names: Duhig, Holly.
Title: Tractor beams / Holly Duhig.
Description: New York : Gareth Stevens Publishing, 2018. | Series:
    Science fiction to science fact | Includes index.
Identifiers: ISBN 9781538214893 (pbk.) | ISBN 9781538213902
    (library bound) | ISBN 9781538214909 (6 pack)
Subjects: LCSH: Lasers--Juvenile literature. | Light--Juvenile
    literature.
Classification: LCC TA1682.D84 2018 | DDC 621.36'6--dc23

Published in 2018 by
Gareth Stevens Publishing
111 East 14th Street, Suite 349
New York, NY 10003

Written by: Holly Duhig
Edited by: John Wood
Designed by: Matt Rumbelow

Photo credits: Abbreviations: l-left, r-right, b-bottom, t-top, c-center, m-middle.
With thanks to Getty Images, Thinkstock Photo and iStockphoto. Cover: bg
– MaxyM; front – Halfpoint. 2 – Fer Gregory. 4 – Algol. 5 – Luadthong. 6
– lassedesignen. 7: t1 – vs148; t2 – ESB Professional. 8: t – Rick Partington;
b – Vadim Sadovski. 9: t – Esteban De Armas; b – Raymond Cassel. 10: l
– Scanrail1; c – MrGarry. 11: t – BalancePhoto; b – tchara. 12: t – dezignor;
b – Aumm graphixphoto. 13: t – 123dartist; b – Andrii Zhezhera. 14 – Mix-
space. 15: t – Yury Zap; b – doomu. 16 – Fer Gregory. 17 – Sylverarts Vectors.
18 – CLUSTERX. 19 – Igor Zh. 20: t – Fotografiche; b – Joshua Jo. 21 – Robert
Kneschke. 22: t – Roman3dAr; b – exopixel. 23 – Marcos Mesa Sam Wordley.
24: bl – solarseven; tr – Stepan Kapl. 25: tr – eurobanks, br – SNP_SS. 26: bg –
Fer Gregory; br – VaLiza. 27: Algo. 28: tr – Quality Master; br Kate Artyukhova.
29: bg – acharyahargreaves; front – Albert Ziganshin. 30: bg – camilkuo;
br – racorn.

Printed in China
CPSIA compliance information: Batch CS18GS: For further information contact
Gareth Stevens, New York, New York at 1-800-542-2595.

SYSTEM
PROTECTION

CONTENTS

Words that appear like this can be found in the glossary on page 31.

TRACTOR BEAMS: THE FANTASY

WHAT IS A TRACTOR BEAM?

A tractor beam is a beam of light that has enough energy to pull things towards its source. In the futuristic world of science fiction, tractor beams are everywhere.

UFOs use them to abduct unsuspecting humans off the face of the planet, and spaceships use them to beam up members of their crew.

They are a popular gadget in television shows such as Star Trek where they are used to tow broken ships to safety, or to capture enemy spaceships. Using two beams of light, the Star Trek-style tractor beams create an interference pattern. The beams are then polarized so that anything from an object or person to a whole spacecraft can be pulled into the beam. Although this sounds like technology of the 22nd century, there is a surprising amount of tractor beam technology alive in the 21st.

3.52

1.41

3.52

SYSTEM
PROTECTION

LOGIN   - - - - - - - - - - - - - - - - - -
PASSWORD   - - - - - - - - - - - - - - -

FIRST NAME: JOE
LAST NAME: SMITH
HISTORY: MISSING
POTENTIALLY
DANGEROUS

SPACE EXPLORATION

It's fun to imagine a future where tractor beams go hand-in-hand with space travel. Flying through space when you find yourself on a collision course with a stray asteroid? Just capture it in your ship's tractor beam and ta-da, problem solved. Run into some unfriendly aliens while exploring a new planet? Just get your crew to beam you straight out of there!

Daydreams aside, did you know America's space agency, NASA, is hoping to use real-life tractor beams to search for life on other planets? Scientists are always discovering planets in distant solar systems, and they have more technology than ever to study them. However, sending spacecraft to distant worlds is still very hard work, and even if we could get one there, it's a bit of a one-way journey. Once we land spacecraft on other planets, there's no getting them back!

The invention of tractor beams would solve this problem completely. With a tractor beam handy, you needn't touch-down on an alien planet at all. We could simply beam up material for our interplanetary investigations and send it straight back to Earth for scientists to study. Who knows what we might find?

Making beams of light strong enough to "beam up" people might seem like humankind's most far-fetched dream, but they are closer to becoming a reality than you might think. In fact, some Earth-bound tractor beams have already been invented that are surprisingly similar to those used in the Star Trek universe.

USEFUL TRACTOR BEAMS

Even here on Earth, being able to use beams of light to move objects would be very useful indeed. Instead of giant space-tractor beams, imagine a future where everybody owned a handheld tractor beam. Need a snack? Just beam it from the kitchen straight into your hands. TV remote too far away? No problem. Just lure it towards you with the power of light!

Never having to leave the couch again would be a dream come true for most of us but scientists seem to think Earth-bound tractor beams could be used for more important things.

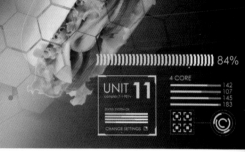

))))))))))))))))))))))))))))))))))))))) 84%

UNIT **11**

4 CORE
142
107
145
183

CHANGE SETTINGS

Tractor beams could allow doctors to perform surgery on sick people without having to cut into them. This could save millions of lives! Tractor beams could also be a hands-free way of removing harmful things from patient's bodies. They may also be used to deliver medicine straight to the part of the body that needs it most. Scientists have already managed to move **microscopic** objects using light. This means they might be able to use tiny tractor beams to study human **DNA** and find cures for many diseases!

TRACTOR BEAMS: THE CHALLENGE

Scientists have been working harder than ever to make tractor beams a reality, but they still face many challenges. The main challenge to tractor beam technology is gravity. Gravity is the force that pulls everything to the center of the Earth. It is the whole reason we don't just float off the planet into outer space. Any technology designed to pull an object towards it has to have a pulling force stronger than Earth's gravity.

Making something that can overcome gravity with the power of light is hard enough on Earth, but what about using tractor beams to explore other planets? All planets have a gravitational pull which can be stronger or weaker depending on their size. Bigger planets have a stronger gravitational pull. For example, to zap something off the surface of Jupiter (the largest planet in our solar system) a tractor beam would have to overcome its gravitational pull – which is twice as strong as Earth's!

PUSH AND PULL

The second problem with tractor beams is light itself. The science fact behind the science fiction goes against everything we know about light. Light is a type of energy. It is made of particles called photons which have a type of movement energy called momentum. This means photons can push objects when they hit them.

LIGHT

In fact, scientists have invented huge, reflective pieces of material called solar sails that unfurl and use light from the Sun to push satellites through space. If we can use the momentum of photons to pull objects, rather than push them, we will be one step closer to unlocking the secret to tractor beams.

LIGHT: THE SCIENCE OF ATTRACTION

To understand how we can use light to pull objects we must first understand a little more about how light works. First of all, light travels in waves. Light that we get from the Sun and lightbulbs is called white light, but it is actually made up of many waves, each of which is a different color. These colors are red, orange, yellow, green, blue, indigo, and violet. Each wave of color has a different wavelength. This is the distance between the same point on two waves.

In fact, light is part of a whole group of waves that make up something called the **electromagnetic spectrum**. The electromagnetic spectrum is also responsible for the radio waves that play your music and the microwaves that heat your food. But our eyes cannot see these waves – they can only see light waves.

WAVE LENGTH

RADIO WAVES

MICROWAVES

VISIBLE LIGHT

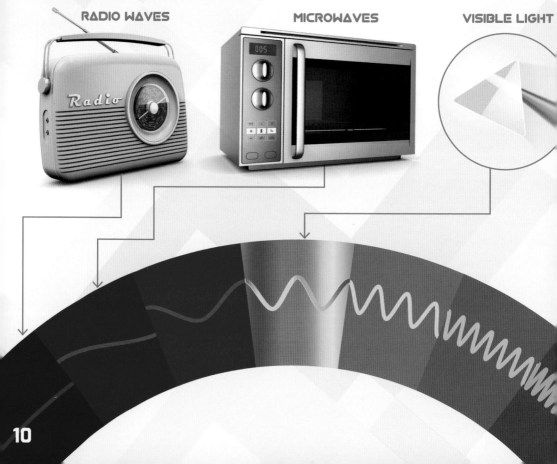

DIFFRACTION

Light waves are able to spread out in all directions. This is why when you turn on a lamp in a dark room, the whole room will light up, and not just the part of the room the lamp is in. This is called diffraction. You can think of light waves like ocean waves. If you dig a hole on the beach and let the water flow into it, you will see that the water spreads out in all directions to fill all of the space in the hole, just like the light in the room.

When light is diffracted, the photons in light also spread out in all directions. This means the farther away light is from its source, the less momentum the light has. That means less push! In their attempts to make a powerful, real-life tractor beam, researchers have to find ways of stopping light from diffracting. By focusing light in one direction, the beam will not diffract and lose its push power as it moves farther away from the light source.

LASERS AND LENSES

One way we can stop diffraction and create a focused tractor beam is by using lasers. Lasers do not diffract as much as normal light. This is because laser light is bounced back and forth between two mirrors facing each other before being shone out of a tiny gap. This helps focus the direction of the light.

You may have seen a laser pointer before. If you have, you will have noticed the light they shine is colored – usually red. If the light is all the same color, it is also the same wavelength. These wavelengths can be lined up next to each other, which makes the laser more powerful. Because they are so powerful, lasers can create a lot of heat. Some lasers can even be used to slice through things by melting, or **vaporizing**, anything they touch.

LASERS CAN BE USED TO CUT THROUGH MATERIALS AS TOUGH AS METAL OR EVEN DIAMOND!

Powerful lasers are a good place to start in the mission to make tractor beams a reality. In fact, scientists are already using laser equipment to pick up and hold tiny particles. The equipment is called "optical tweezers."

Optical tweezers work by shining a powerful laser through a glass lens. This lens is a convex lens. This means that it bulges out in the middle. When rays of light pass through a convex lens, they are bent inwards and focused towards a single point called the focal point. Optical tweezers trap particles in the focal point because the light is strongest there.

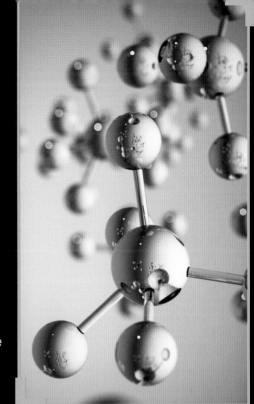

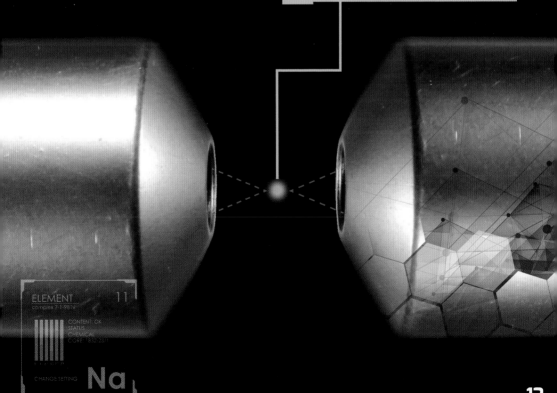

ELEMENT 11
complex 7-1-981V

CONTENT: OK
STATUS
CHEMICAL
CORE: 832-2311

CHANGE SETTING Na

THE BESSEL BEAM

Lasers are a good place to start if we want to make light strong enough to make a tractor beam, but they do have their drawbacks. Firstly, although lasers diffract less light than normal light sources, they do still diffract a bit. In fact, if you pointed a laser at the moon, the red dot that would appear on it would be bigger than the moon itself!

But don't be disheartened. Science has a solution. If you point a laser at a wall, it will appear as one red dot. But if you point a Bessel beam at a wall, it will appear as a red dot with lots of rings around it – like when you throw a stone into a pond. Bessel beams are light beams that behave very differently from lasers. The main difference between a laser and a Bessel beam is that Bessel beams diffract much less light.

3.52

1.41

Bessel beams are made by overlapping the light of two lasers. Because lasers are made of one wavelength (color) of light, when we overlap them, the light waves that cross over each other are the same size.

Bessel beams are small, narrow, and very strong. Because of this, they can be used like needles. A needle made of light might sound like a crazy idea, but it can be very useful. For example, Bessel beams can be used to pierce things as small as a single human cell. Cells make up your whole body and most of them are so small they can only be seen under a microscope.

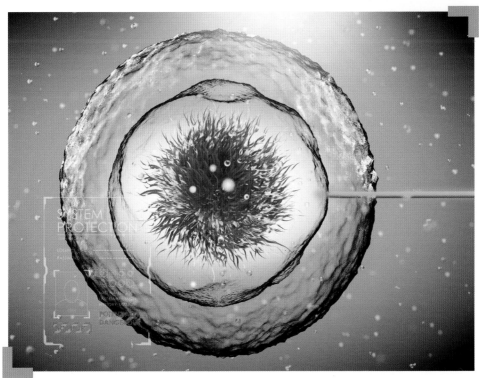

THE CONVEYOR BEAM

So how are Bessel beams being used in the invention of tractor beams? Well, top researchers have found a way to use Bessel beams to make a tractor beam that acts like a conveyor belt. Sounds useful, right? Imagine things being pulled toward you in a tractor beam just as easily as your groceries are pulled along the conveyor belt at checkout.

What's more, this tractor beam works in a very similar way to the tractor beams of science fiction. This is because, just like in Star Trek, the optical conveyor beam uses two overlapping beams to create an interference pattern. Could this be the answer science has been looking for?

INTERFERENCE PATTERNS

Interference patterns have opened a whole new door for tractor beam technology, but what exactly are they and how are they made?

Interference patterns in light are created when two beams of light overlap and the light waves **interact**. The highest point of a wave is called the peak, and the lowest point is called the trough. When the peaks and troughs of one wave line up with the peaks and troughs of another, the light becomes extra bright. However, sometimes the peaks of one wave will line up with the troughs of another. When this happens, the light waves cancel each other out and the result is darkness. The inventors of the optical conveyor beam discovered that when this happens all at once, it creates a pattern of flashing lights that can hold small particles.

NO INTERFERENCE

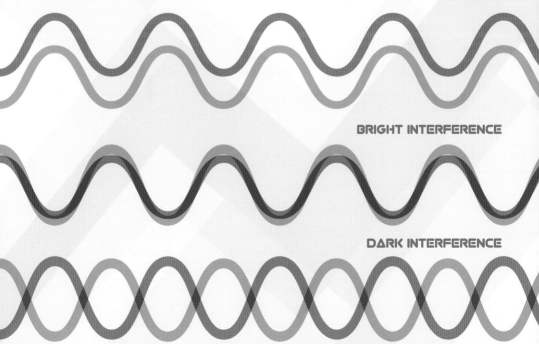

BRIGHT INTERFERENCE

DARK INTERFERENCE

Researchers direct the Bessel beams using glass lenses. This helps create the interference pattern that the particle is placed in. But what makes this attempt any different from optical tweezers? Well, the optical conveyor beam doesn't just hold the particle – it can move it too! In fact, the conveyor beam can be used to pull objects just like a real, working tractor beam!

This is because the particle is drawn up into the light patches of the interference pattern. As these light patches dance around, the particle moves with them.

ELEMENT   11
complex 7-1-981v

CONTENT: OK
STATUS
CHEMICAL
CORE: 1632-23/1

81 42 11 30 67 59

CHANGE SETTING   Na

Sounds great, right? We've nailed it. A real-life tractor beam! Well, not quite. This tractor beam does work but has many downsides. First of all, the beam is only able to move things smaller than the wavelengths of light. This means it can only be used to drag tiny particles. Secondly, this tractor beam has only been able to pull a particle forward by a few micrometers. A micrometer is one millionth of a meter. That won't get us very far!

Lastly, the biggest problem with the conveyor beam is that it needs lots of energy. To make Bessel beams strong enough to lift everyday objects or even people would require an **infinite** amount of energy, which is just not possible. Even if it was, a Bessel beam this strong would be so hot that it would destroy you, so we can definitely count this one out!

THE SOLENOID BEAM

As we know, light gives a pushing force when it hits an object. We also know that this is not very helpful for tractor beams, which need to pull objects using light alone. Another problem is that objects block rays of light. When light hits an object, it is blocked, and a shadow in the shape of the object is cast. Your own shadow is a result of the light from the Sun and other sources being blocked by your body.

Luckily, scientists have succeeded in inventing a different kind of tractor beam altogether. The solenoid beam allows light to travel past an object instead of hitting it. This means the light doesn't lose its momentum. They then discovered they could angle the light so that it could push a particle up from underneath. But just how does this work?

Once again, Bessel beams had a part to play in this. Bessel beams aren't blocked by objects. When an object is placed in the path of a Bessel beam, the light is not blocked – only interrupted until it can reform on the other side of the object.

Researchers discovered that the reformed light could be used to hit a particle from underneath. This way, the light could bounce the object in the opposite direction – back towards the light source. But how did they manage this?

SPIRALS OF LIGHT

This is where the clever stuff comes in. Researchers found a way of directing light into a spiral shape with a hollow center. You can think of this spiral of light like a corkscrew. The spiral shape of a corkscrew allows it to pull a cork out of a bottle as it twists around. In the same way, the light in a solenoid beam lifts particles up from underneath as it twists.

Granted, this spiral shape would look a bit different from the green shafts of light that we're used to seeing in science fiction. But being spiraled up into space sounds pretty exciting too!

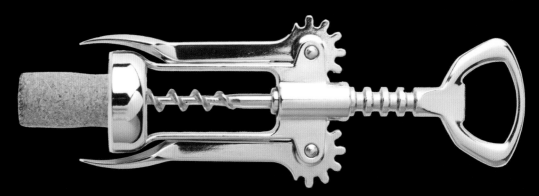

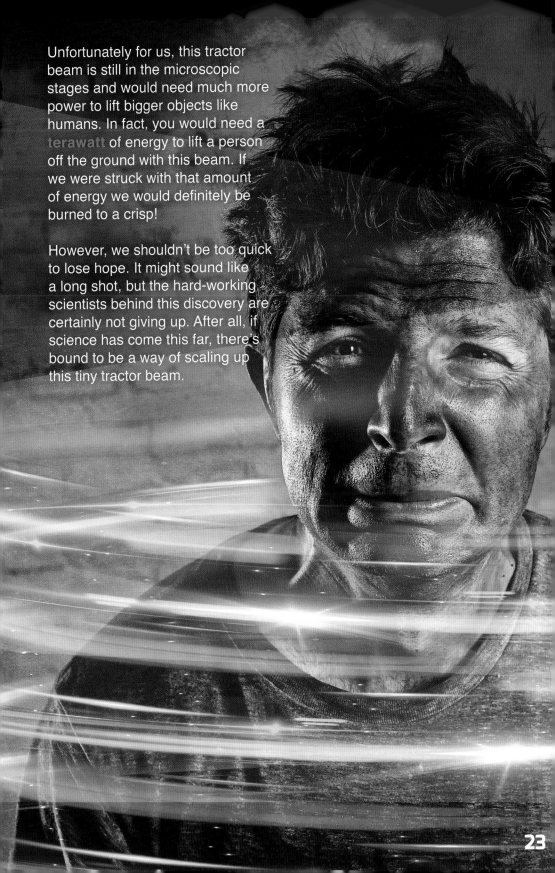

Unfortunately for us, this tractor beam is still in the microscopic stages and would need much more power to lift bigger objects like humans. In fact, you would need a terawatt of energy to lift a person off the ground with this beam. If we were struck with that amount of energy we would definitely be burned to a crisp!

However, we shouldn't be too quick to lose hope. It might sound like a long shot, but the hard-working scientists behind this discovery are certainly not giving up. After all, if science has come this far, there's bound to be a way of scaling up this tiny tractor beam.

THE SONIC BEAM

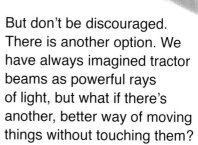

Unfortunately, there seems to be many things standing in the way of our favorite piece of fictional technology becoming a reality. The attempts we've seen so far use too much energy, destroy us, and only seem to be able to move microscopic particles.

But don't be discouraged. There is another option. We have always imagined tractor beams as powerful rays of light, but what if there's another, better way of moving things without touching them?

Luckily for us, one group of scientists began to think outside the box and invented a device that can levitate and move objects with sound! In what they call a sonic tractor beam, they have managed to trap and move small beads in an invisible, sonic force field.

SOUND SCIENCE

Pitch is measured in hertz (Hz). The higher the number of hertz, the higher pitched the sound. Human ears can only hear sounds below 20 kilohertz (kHz).

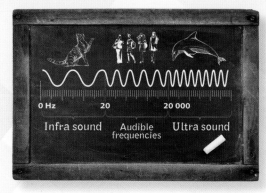

To make a sonic tractor beam, the scientists use a block of 64 loudspeakers to play sounds over 40 kHz. This created an interference pattern of sound which acts as a 3-D force field that can grip and move small beads like an invisible finger and thumb.

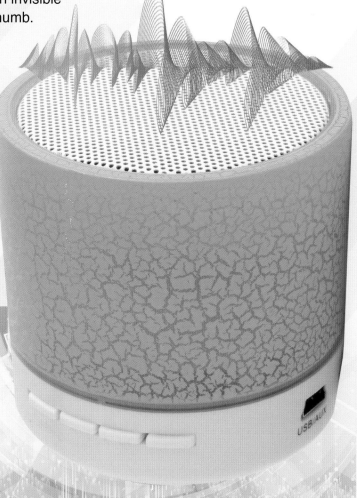

THE PROS AND THE CONS

In more ways than one, this is the best tractor beam design yet. To start with, it can move objects in all directions: side to side, back to front, up and down. It can even spin them around. What's more, the sonic tractor beam doesn't just work on microscopic particles. It can be used to move objects we can actually see. The sonic tractor beam has already been made into a handheld device!

However, like all these noble attempts at turning science fiction into science fact, this design has its drawbacks. First, in order to work, the object being pulled needs to be smaller than the wavelength of sound passing over it. This creates problems when scaling up the sonic beam. To beam up larger objects, the device would need to play sounds with longer wavelengths. If the device played sounds with wavelengths longer than 20kHz, we would be able to hear it, and because the device plays sounds at such a high intensity, it would likely blast our ears off!

We can also wave goodbye to exploring the galaxy with Star Trek-style technology, because these tractor beams wouldn't work in space. This is because sound travels through particles, and there are no particles in space for sound to travel through. Sound is made when particles **vibrate**. When one particle vibrates, it hits the particle next to it which, in turn, begins to vibrate.

If you knock on a wooden door, it makes a sound because your hand is causing the particles in the wood to vibrate.

No particles, no sound. No sound, no sonic tractor beam. It seems the day we use tractor beams in outer space is still a long way off, but hopefully, it won't be as long before you are unwrapping the latest handheld sonic tractor beam for your birthday.

TRACTOR BEAMS: THE FUTURE
ON EARTH

So, what does the future hold for us science fiction fans? Will we have to abandon the idea of sonic tractor beams and work on making light beams that can be used as a pick-up and drop-off service in space?

Perhaps, but let's not be hasty. Tractor beams could have lots of uses here on Earth. For example, they could be used to save lives and help people in trouble. Imagine a world where lifeguards use tractor beams to rescue people from drowning in the ocean. Much quicker than using a lifeboat and much less dangerous than diving in to save them yourself!

We could even use tractor beams to help people in places that have been hit by an earthquake or tornado. These disasters often cause buildings to crumble and people to get trapped underneath them. If we could lift up all the **rubble** in a tractor beam we could rescue the people who might be buried. If we had enough warning and a powerful enough tractor beam, we might even be able to lift everyone to safety before disaster strikes!

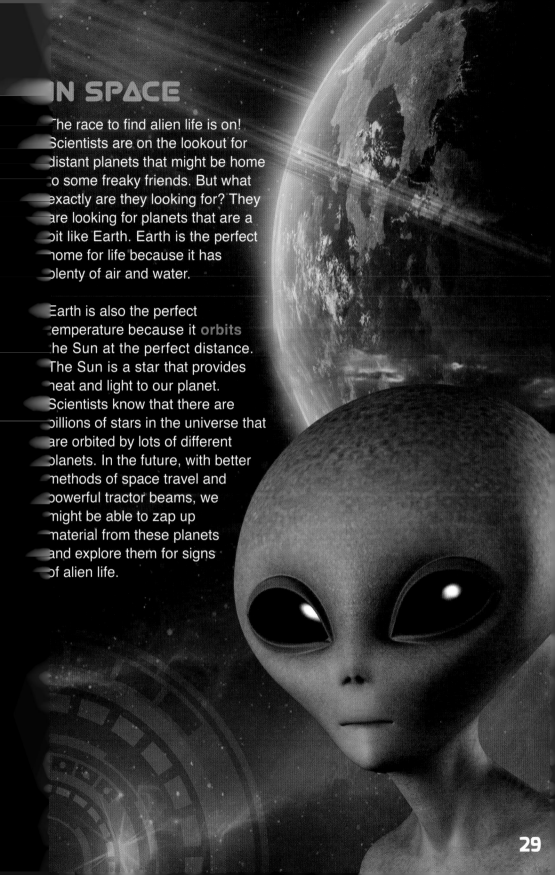

IN SPACE

The race to find alien life is on! Scientists are on the lookout for distant planets that might be home to some freaky friends. But what exactly are they looking for? They are looking for planets that are a bit like Earth. Earth is the perfect home for life because it has plenty of air and water.

Earth is also the perfect temperature because it **orbits** the Sun at the perfect distance. The Sun is a star that provides heat and light to our planet. Scientists know that there are billions of stars in the universe that are orbited by lots of different planets. In the future, with better methods of space travel and powerful tractor beams, we might be able to zap up material from these planets and explore them for signs of alien life.

WRITE YOUR OWN SCIENCE FICTION

If aliens really are out there, there's a chance they will have beaten us to it. They might already be using their own tractor beams to abduct innocent Earthlings. They could even be zapping up our world leaders and beaming down their own kind to take their places.

Or perhaps even scanning their brains, wiping their memories, and dropping them back to Earth as alien slaves. If this has sparked your imagination, why not try writing some science fiction of your own? Who knows? One day it might be science fact.

GLOSSARY

3-D	an object which has height, width and depth
asteroid	rocky and irregularly shaped objects that orbit around the Sun
DNA	a substance that carries information in the cells of plants, humans and animals.
electromagnetic spectrum	the range of waves created by association of electric and magnetic forces
hollow	having a hole or empty space in the middle
infinite	an immeasurable amount
intensity	the strength or power of something
interact	communicate and have an effect on each other
interference pattern	An overall pattern that results when two or more waves interfere with each other
levitate	to rise or hover
microscope	an instrument used by scientists to see very small things
microscopic	so small it can only be viewed under a microscope
orbits	makes a path around a larger object in space
particles	extremely small pieces of a substance
pierce	to go in or through something
polarized	made so that all the vibrations in a light wave take place on one plane
rubble	broken fragments resulting from the destruction of a building
satellites	machines in space that travel around planets, take photographs and collect and transmit information
terawatt	a unit of power equal to one trillion watts
vaporizing	to cause something to turn into a gas-like substance
vibrate	to make small, shaking movements

INDEX